PIANO
LESSON
MADE EASY

LEVEL 1

Lina Ng

Let's move on together for a more "MUSICAL" music education for the new generation.
The ART of Teaching (AoT) is very much suited to be used alongside all piano tutor books and graded syllabus.
Everything in music is interconnected.
You may play the **Musical Moments** series for more **making connections ideas and activities**.

© RHYTHM MP SDN. BHD. 1992
New Edition: 2000

Published by
RHYTHM MP SDN. BHD.
1947, Lorong IKS Bukit Minyak 2,
Taman IKS Bukit Minyak, 14100 Simpang Ampat,
Penang, Malaysia.
Tel: +60 4 5050246 (Direct Line), +60 4 5073690 (Hunting Line)
E-mail: RhythmMP@mphsb.com
Website: www.RhythmMP.com
Follow us on Facebook.com/MusicJamboree

Cover Design & Illustrations by
LIM WAI FUN

ISBN 967-985-361-6
Order No.: MPP-4002-01

Photocopying Prohibited.
All rights reserved. Unauthorised reproduction
of any part of this publication by any means
including photocopying is an infringement of copyright.

Contents

03	Note		32	The Little Finger - R.H.
04	Introduction		33	Worksheet 4, 5
05	C	$\frac{4}{4}$	35	Here We Are — allegro
06	CD		36	Old MacDonald
07	CDE		37	Name The Songs - (1)
09	Mary Had A Little Lamb — mf		38	Yankee Doodle — allegretto
10	Worksheet 1 - notes		39	Mulberry Bush
11	CB		40	Finger Drill - L.H.
12	CBA — dotted minim, $\frac{3}{4}$		41	Chan Mali Chan — ‖ ‖
13	CBAG		42	Row Your Boat — moderato, mp
14	Westminster Chimes		43	Worksheet 6
15	Jala-Jala Ikan		44	Daisy Belle
16	London Bridge		45	Red River Valley — lento
17	Twinkle Twinkle Little Star — p, f		46	On Top Of Old Smoky
18	Worksheet 2		47	Easy Waltz — legato
19	CDEF		48	Worksheet 7 — quaver
20	CDEFG		49	Jingle Bells
21	Ode To Joy		50	Banks Of The Ohio
22	Ker Ren Lai		51	Ten Little Indians
23	Finger Drill - R.H.		52	This Old Man
24	Good Morning		53	Merry Christmas
25	Worksheet 3		54	Clementine
26	Lightly Row — slur		55	Worksheet 8
27	Telefon Ku		56	Name The Songs - (2)
28	Finger Drill - R.H.			
29	French Child's Song			
30	In May			
31	The Saints — tie			

NOTE

1. In the Contents Page, items introduced for the first time has been listed out, to give a specific idea of the contents of the book.

2. Some Oral Work has been included. Mark with a tick when pupil has successfully answered the question.

3. Worksheets are included to :   introduce new items.
   check on the progress of the pupil.
   summarise what has been taught.

4. On pages 37 and 56, if pupil cannot name the song because of language problem, he should try to identify the song by referring to the actual page. The aim is to provide some form of picture recognition activity.

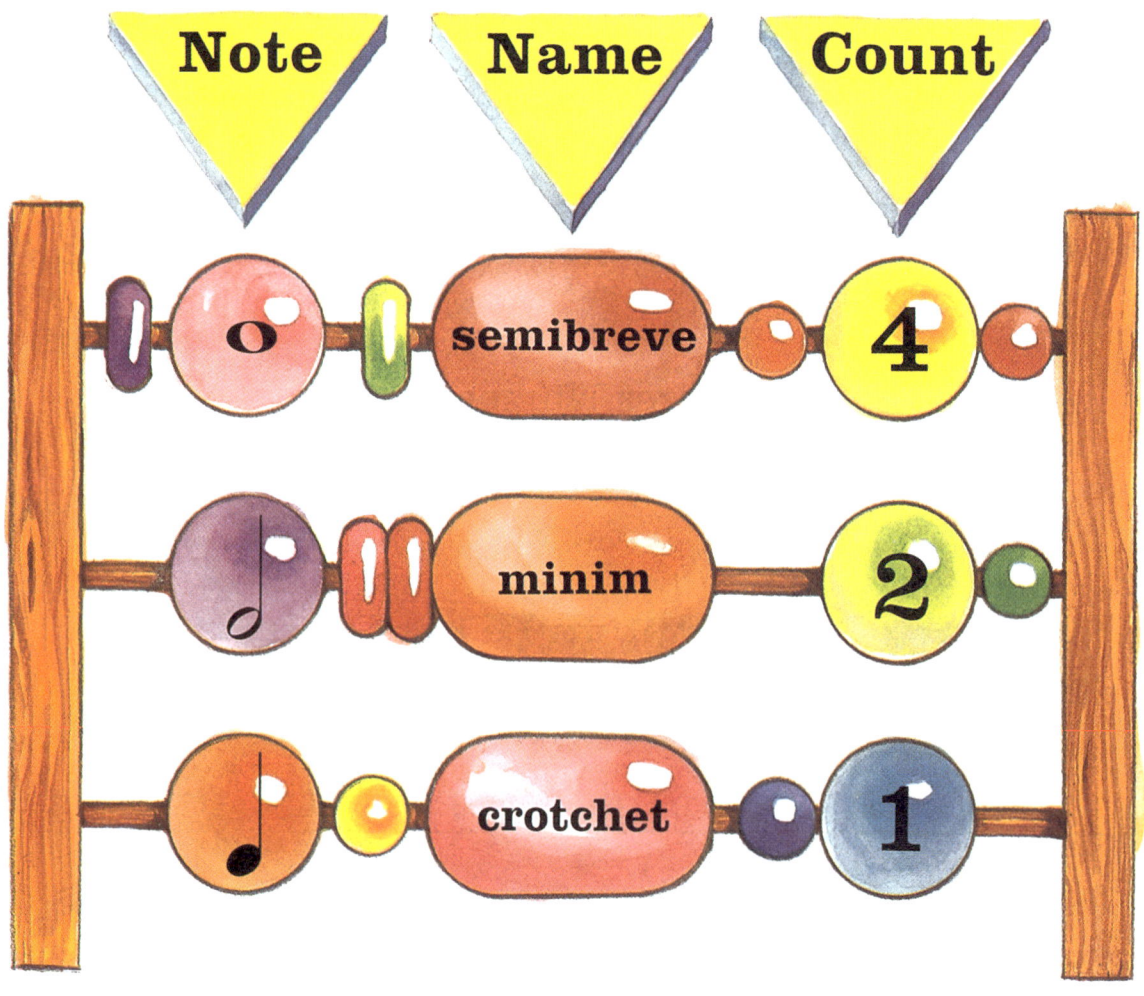

Let's Play C

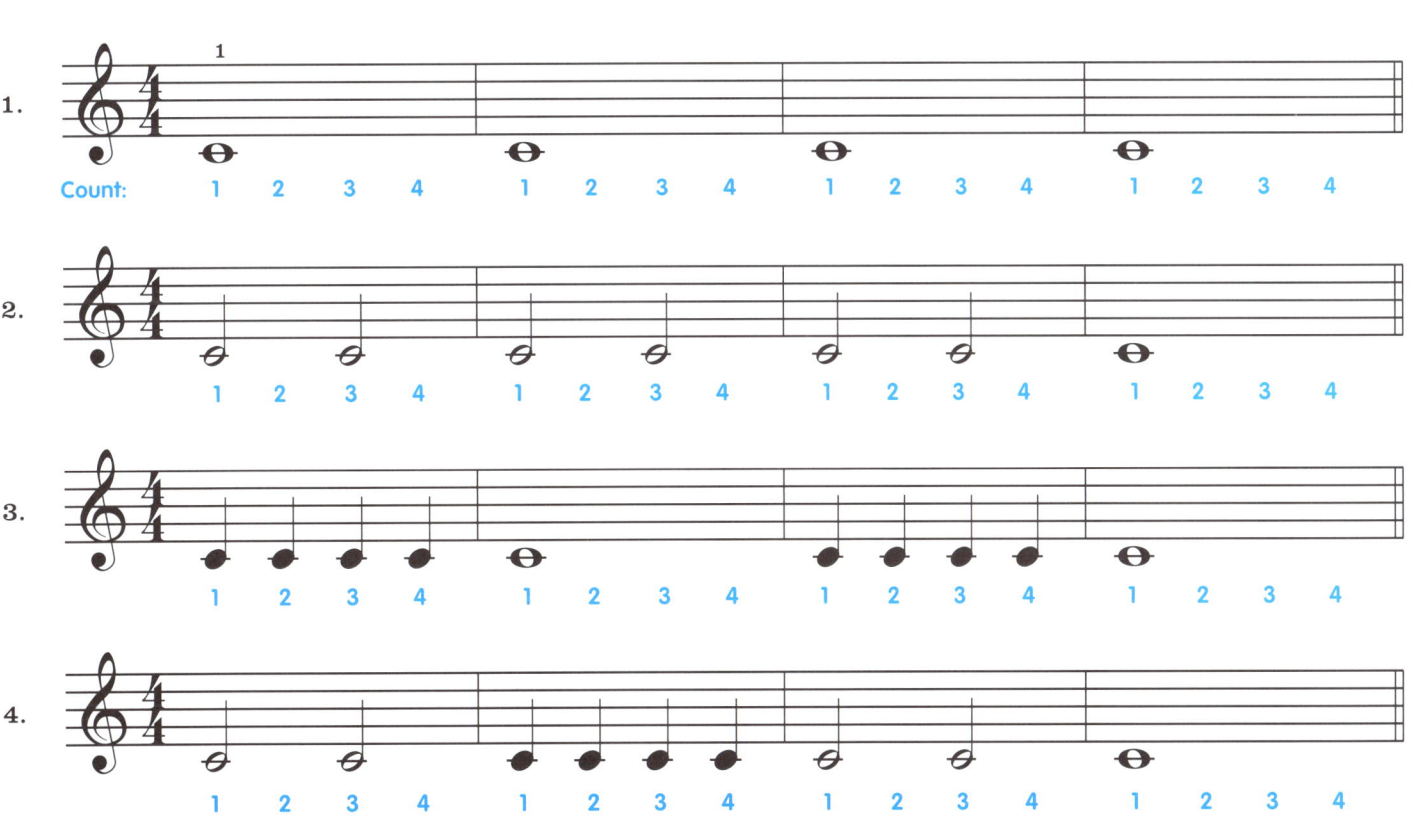

Oral work - Name the notes: semibreve, minim, crotchet.

Let's Play C D

Let's Play C D E

Oral work - Name the notes: C D E.

More Exercises On C D E

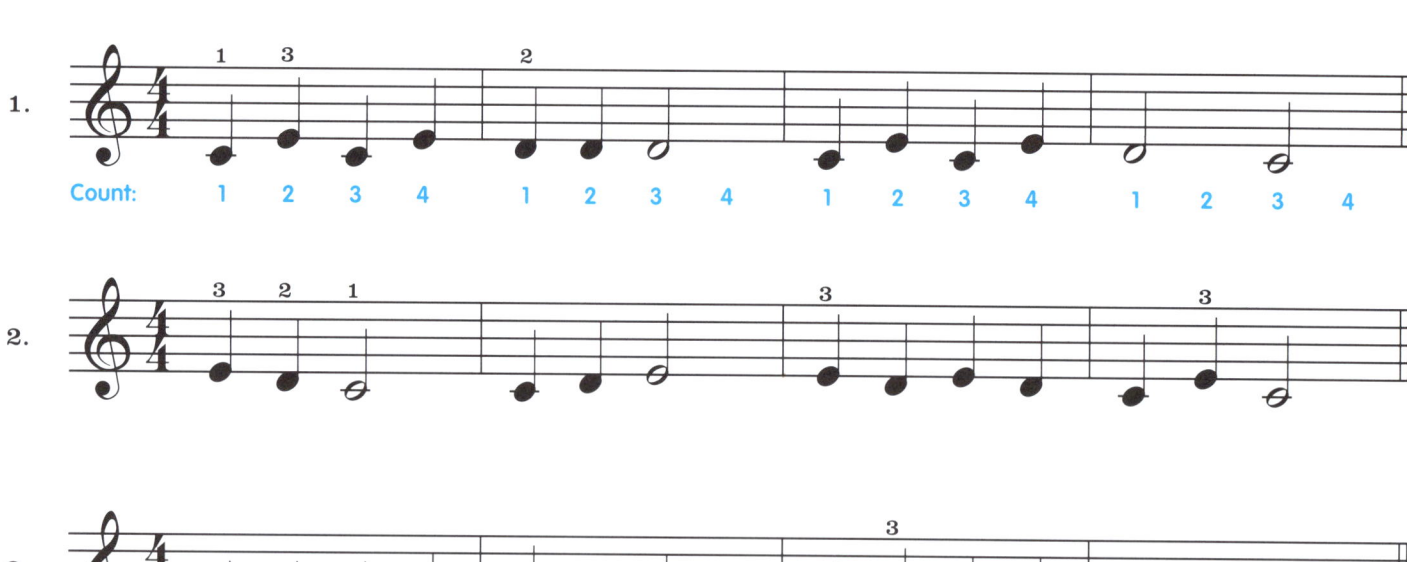

Oral work - Name the notes: semibreve, minim, crotchet. ☐

Give the number of counts: 4, 2, 1. ☐

Name the notes: C D E. ☐

Dynamic Sign

mf (mezzo forte) = moderately loud

Mary Had A Little Lamb

Ma - ry had a lit - tle lamb, lit - tle lamb lit - tle lamb,

mf

Ma - ry had a lit - tle lamb its fleece was white as snow.

Oral work - Sing.

- What does *mf* stand for?

- How should you play it?

Level 1

Worksheet 1

1. Write the counts. (1, 2, 4)

2. Name the notes. (C D E)

3. Insert the counts.

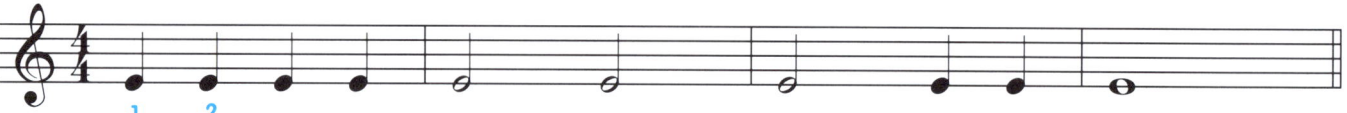

4. Match the note on the stave to the keyboard note.

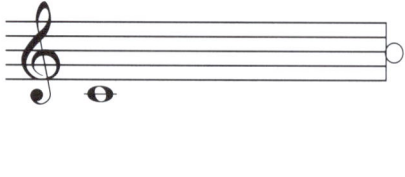   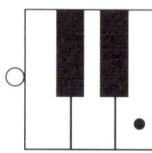

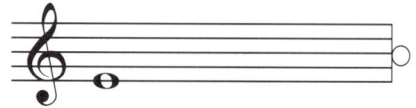   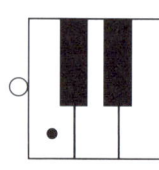

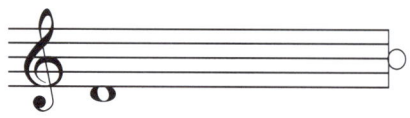   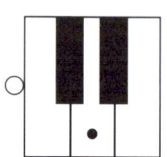

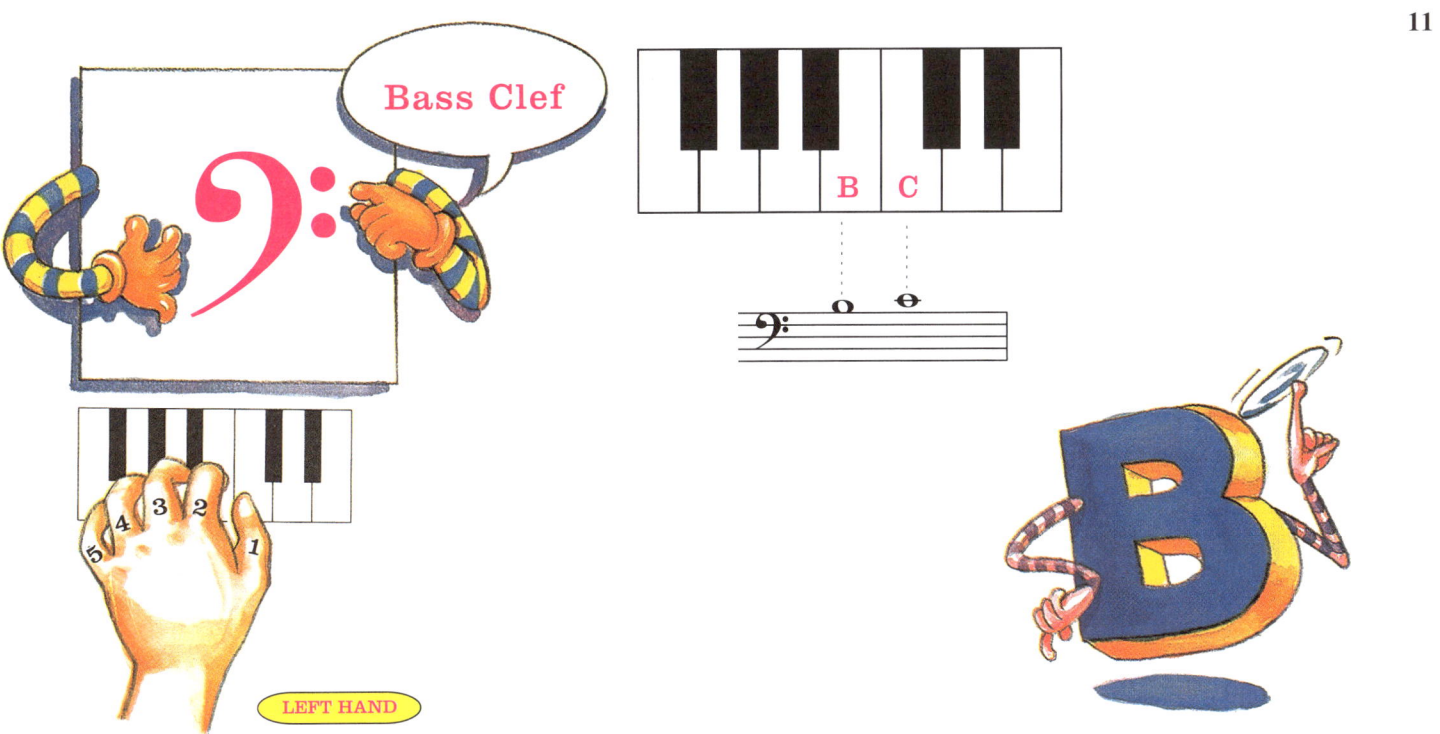

Let's Play C B

You may now begin "Finger Exercises Made Easy - Level 1" for more exercises and sight-reading.

Let's Play C B A G

1. 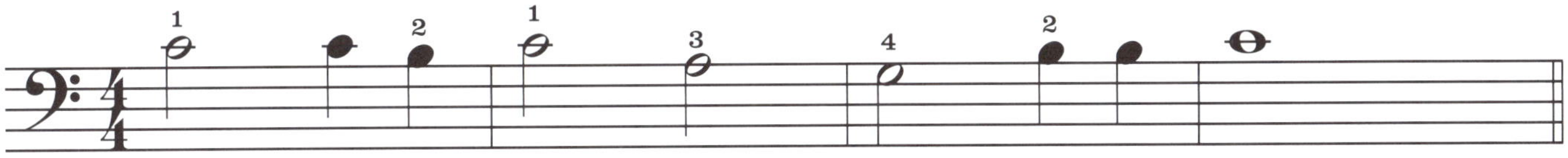
2. 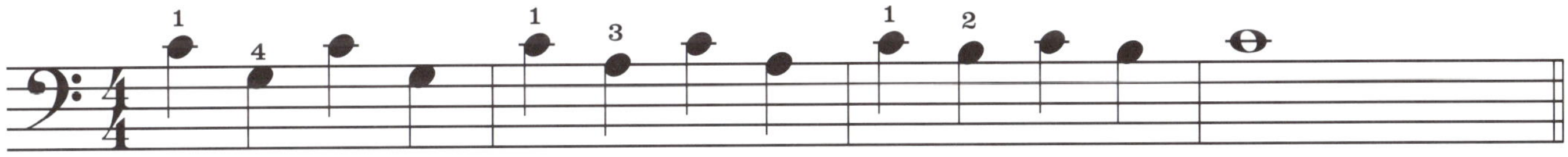
3. 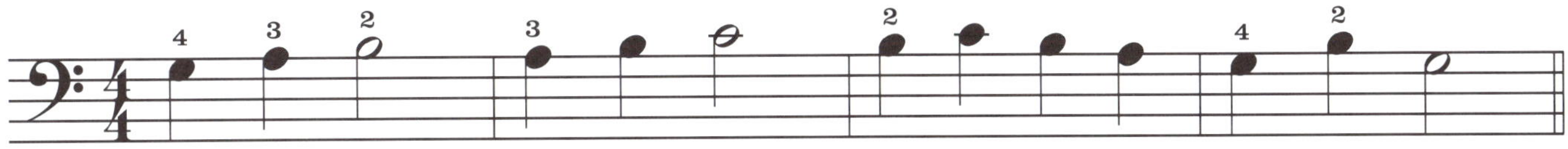
4. 
5.

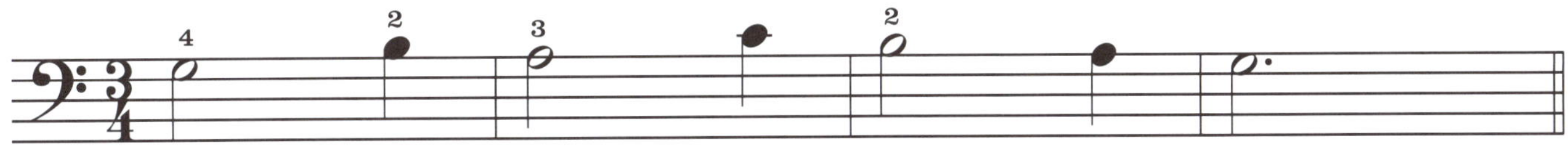

Oral work - Name the notes: C B A G.

Level 1

Now, let us play with both hands.

Westminster Chimes

(Time Signature)

Oral work - What is the time signature?

What are the 4 notes you play here?

Level 1

mf (mezzo forte) = moderately loud

Jala - Jala Ikan
(Malay Song)

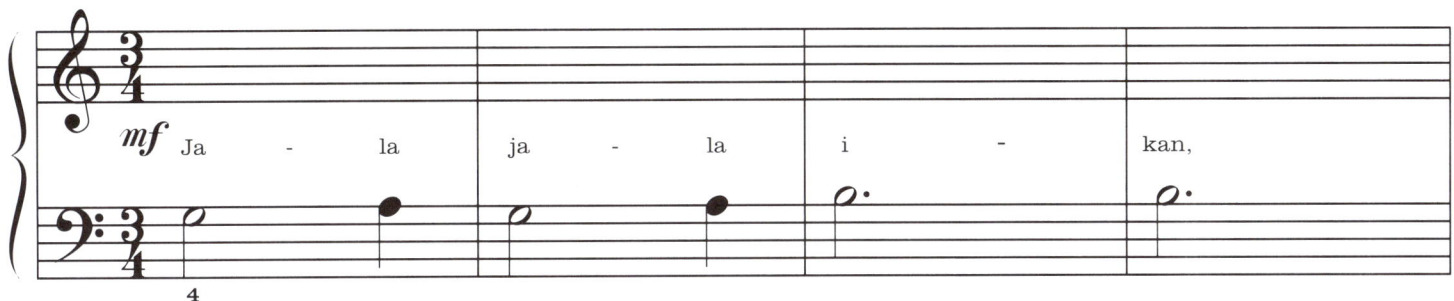
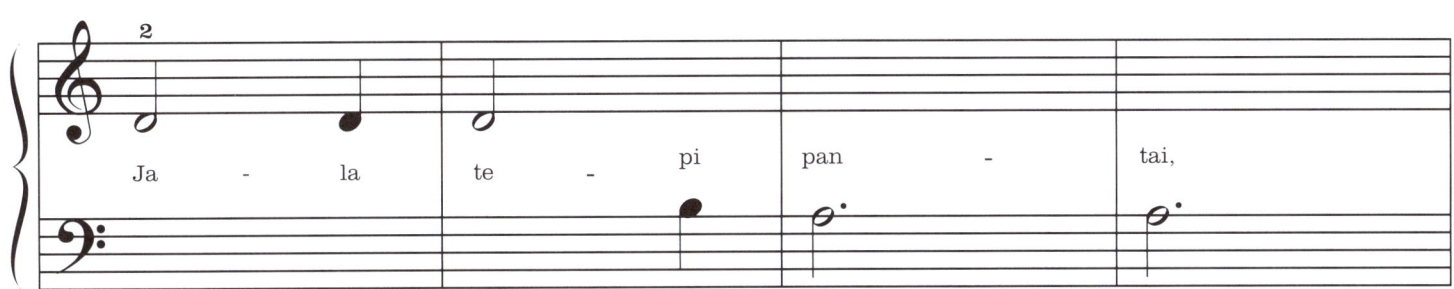
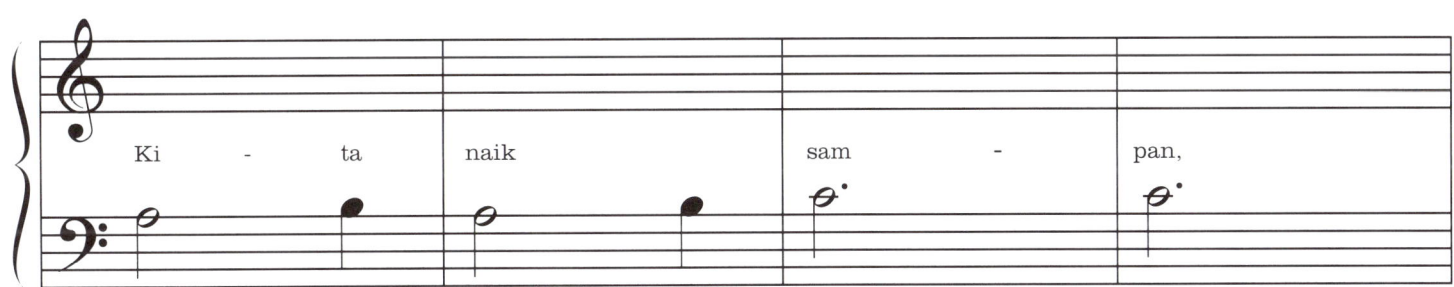
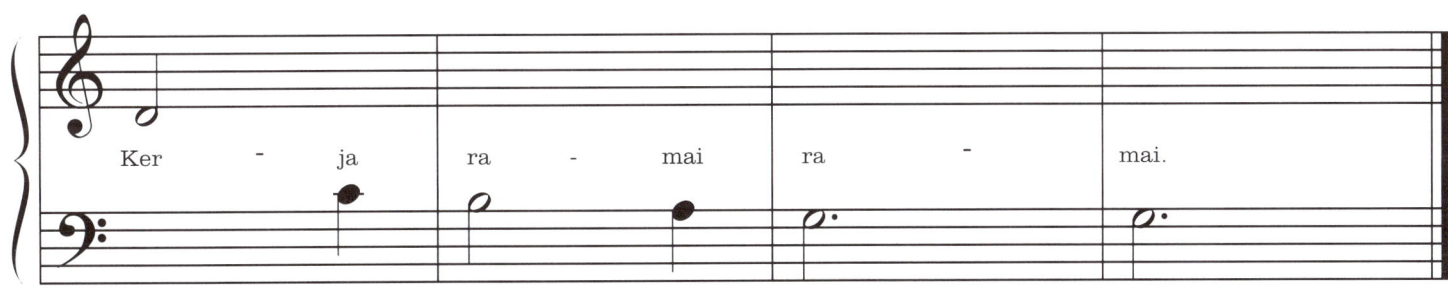

Oral work - What is the time signature? ☐

How loud should you play this piece? ☐

London Bridge

Oral work - What is the time signature here? ☐

How many counts are there in each bar? ☐

Dynamic Sign
p (piano) = soft
f (forte) = loud

Twinkle Twinkle Little Star

French Folk Tune

f Twin-kle Twin-kle lit-tle star, *p* How I won-der what you are,
f Up a-bove the world so high, *p* Like a dia-mond in the sky,
f Twin-kle Twin-kle lit-tle star, *p* How I won-der what you are.

Oral work - What are the new dynamic signs here?

Level 1

Worksheet 2

1. Circle the correct time signature.

2. Name the notes.

C _ _ _   _ _ _ _

3. Insert the counts.

Let's Play C D E F

Let's Play C D E F G

Ode To Joy

Beethoven

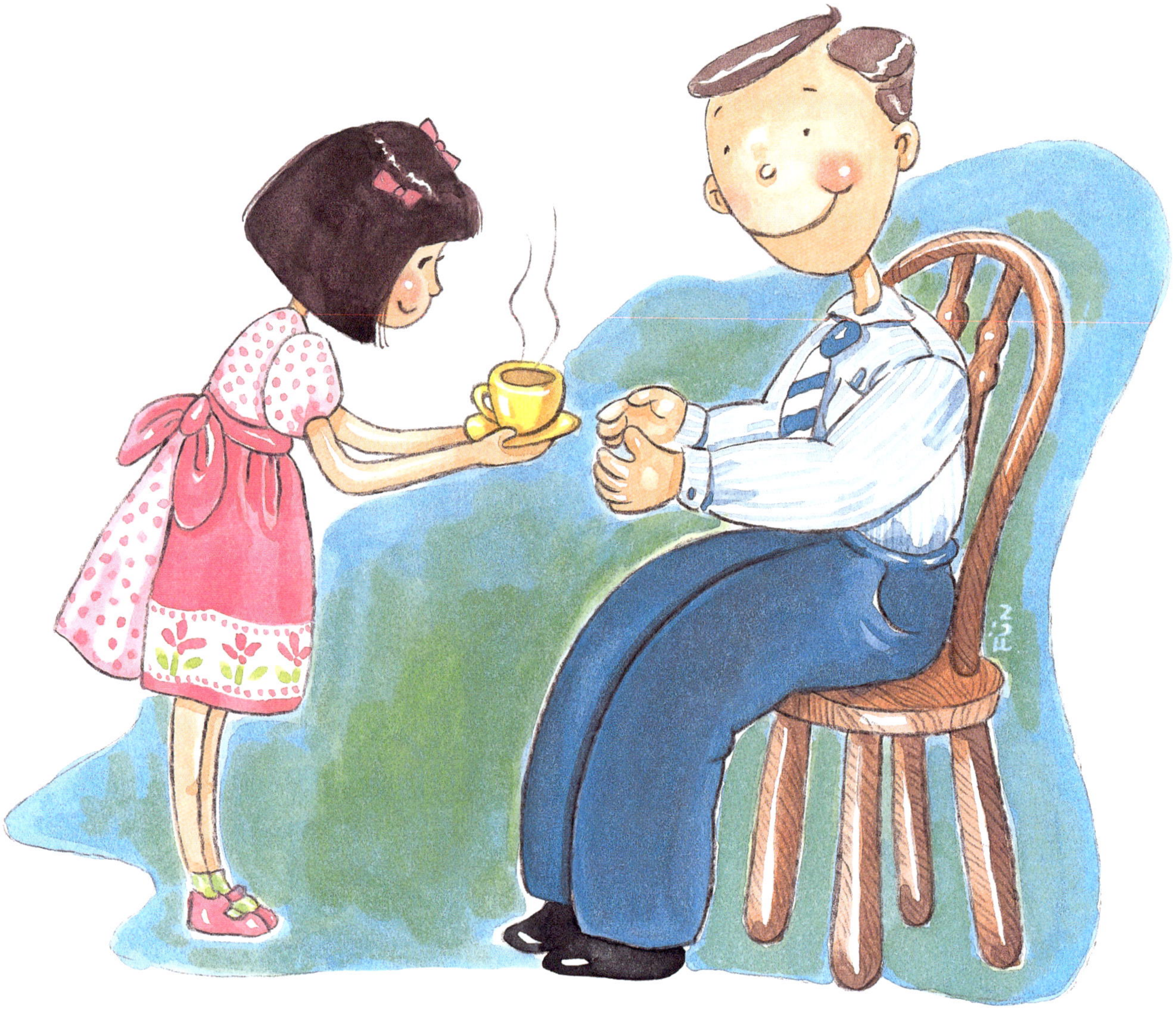

Ker Ren Lai

(Chinese Song)

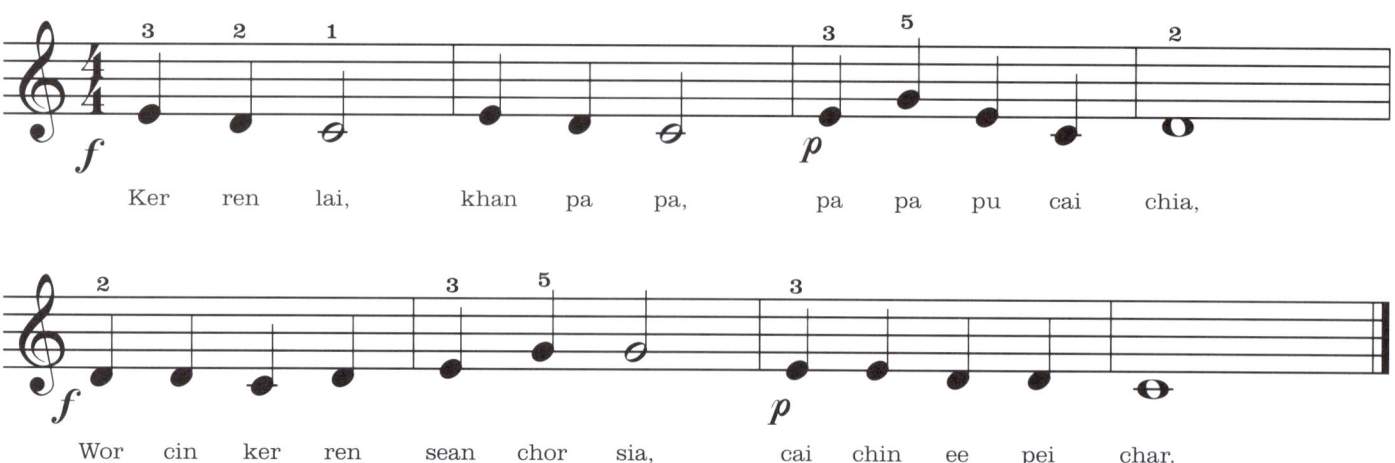

3 2 1 3 5 2
f p
Ker ren lai, khan pa pa, pa pa pu cai chia,
2 3 5 3
f p
Wor cin ker ren sean chor sia, cai chin ee pei char.

Finger Drill
(R.H.)

Good Morning

Good morn-ing, Good morn-ing, Nice to see your smil-ing face;

Good morn-ing, Good morn-ing, To you and to you.

Hel-lo Ben Jee, Hel-lo John, Hel-lo Ten Nee, Hel-lo Tom;

Good morn-ing, Good morn-ing, To you and to you.

WORKSHEET 3

1. Indicate on the keyboard the notes to be played.

 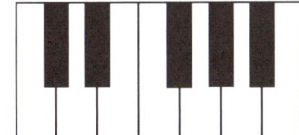

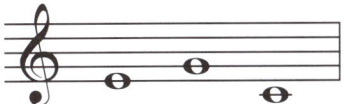 

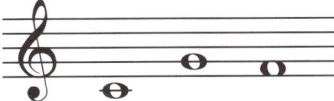 

2. Insert the fingering for the following. (1, 2, 3, 4, 5)

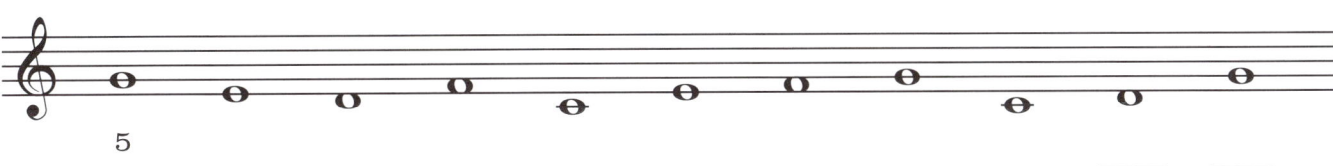

Level 1

(slur) - play smoothly but lift fingers off the keyboard at the end of the slur.

Lightly Row

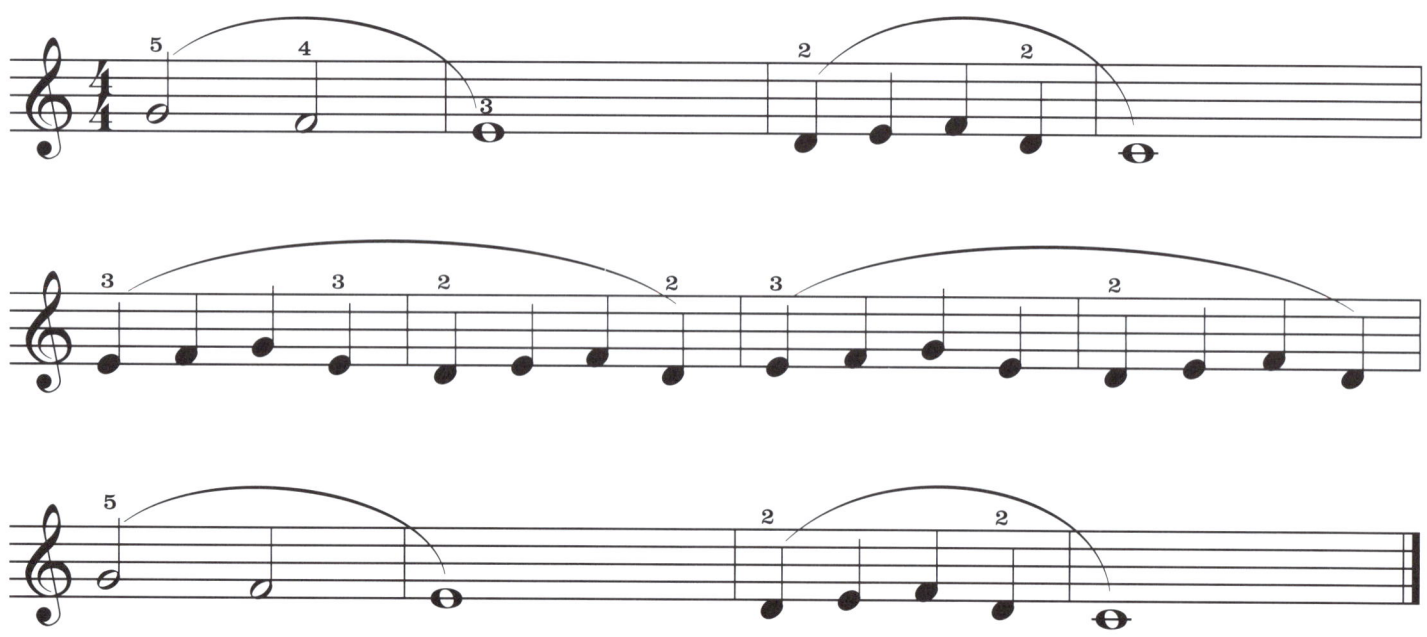

RING... HELLOO.. RING..

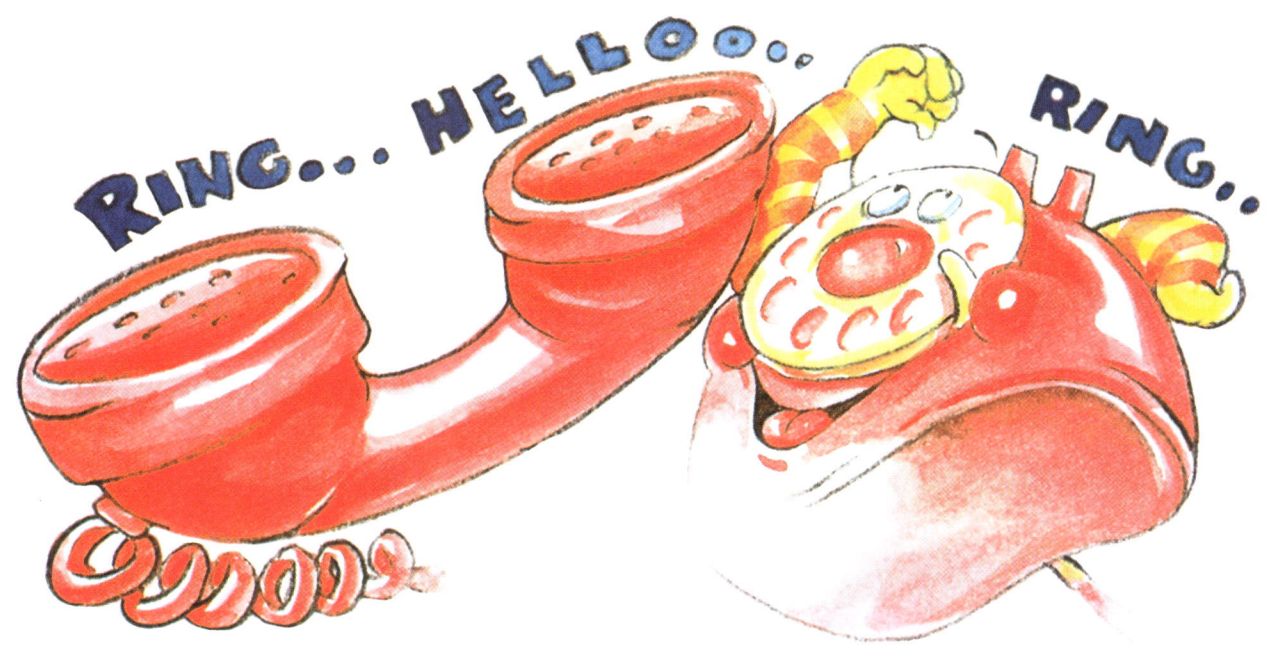

Telefon Ku
(Malay Song)

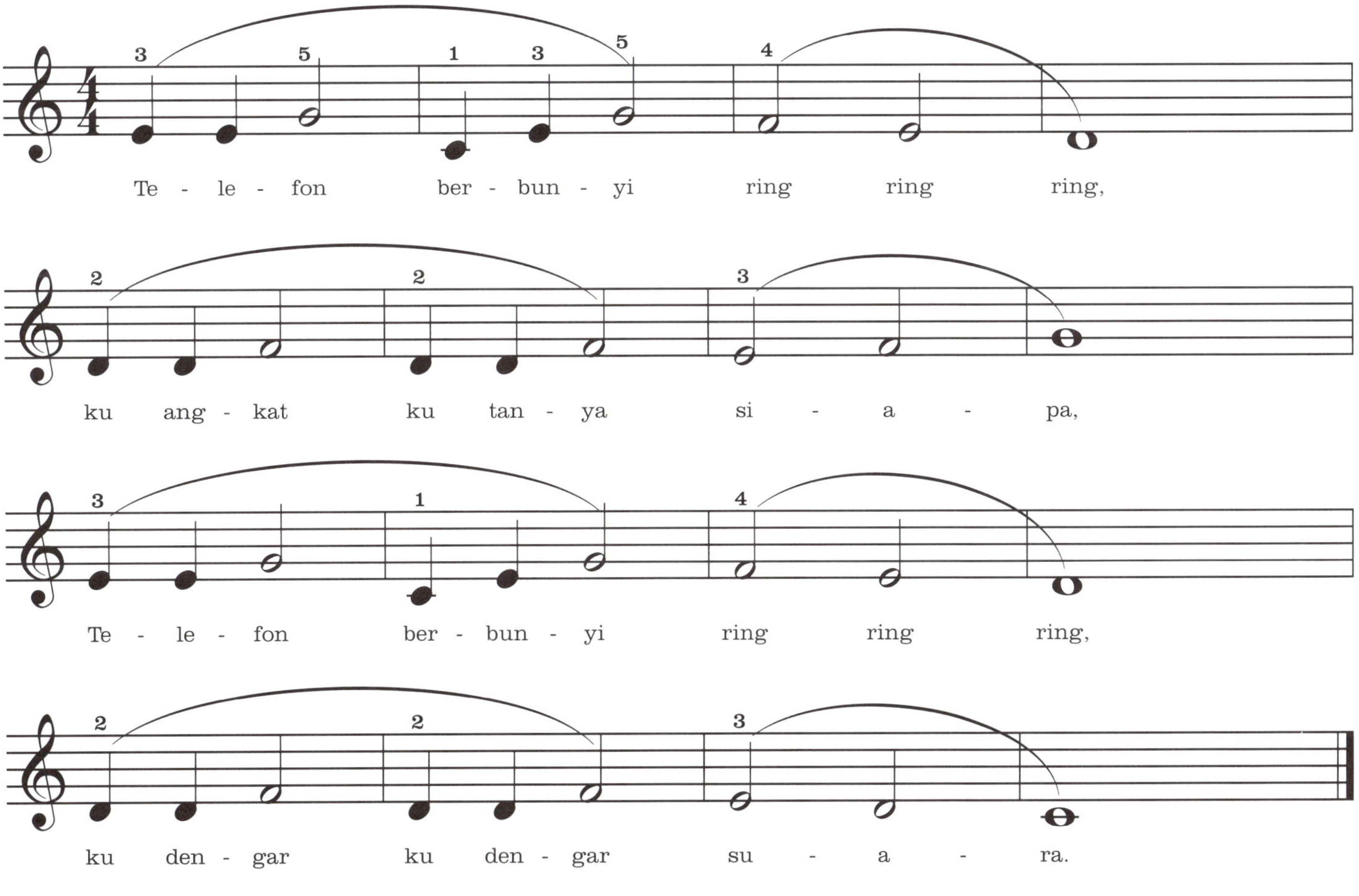
Te - le - fon ber - bun - yi ring ring ring,
ku ang - kat ku tan - ya si - a - pa,
Te - le - fon ber - bun - yi ring ring ring,
ku den - gar ku den - gar su - a - ra.

Finger Drill
(R.H.)

French Child's Song

Franz Behr

Play and count

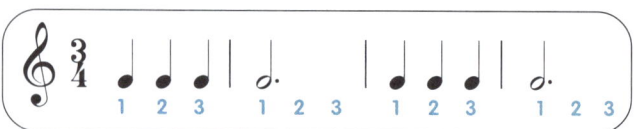

In May

Franz Behr

Tie

1 2 3 4 1

Hold the note for 5 counts.
Count: 12341

1 2 3 4 1

Hold the note for 6 counts.
Count: 123412

The Saints

Traditional

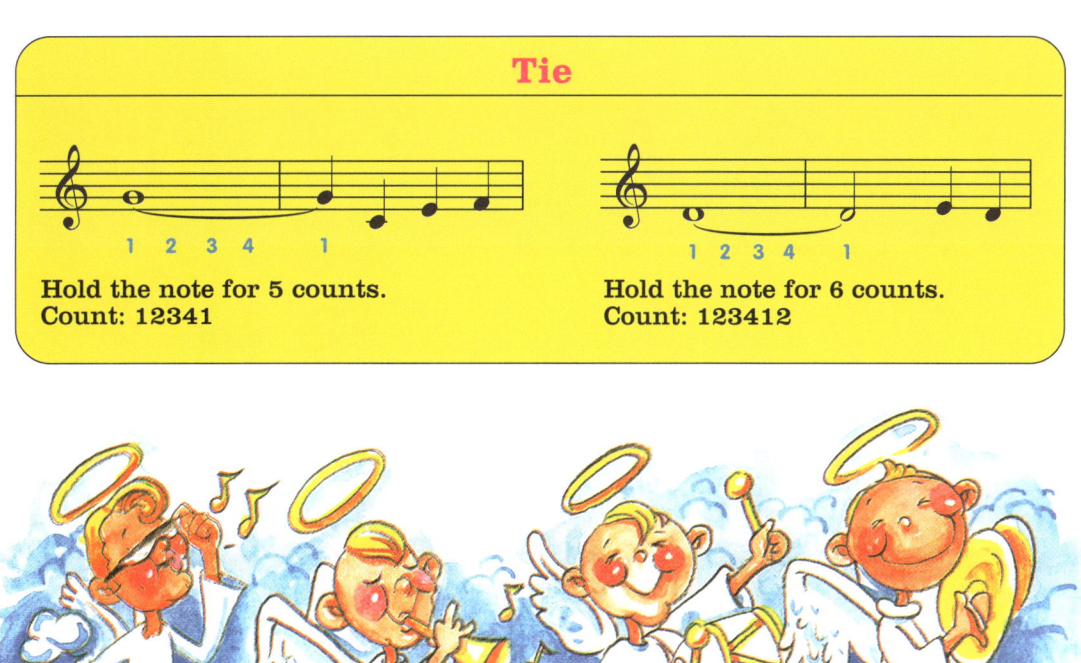

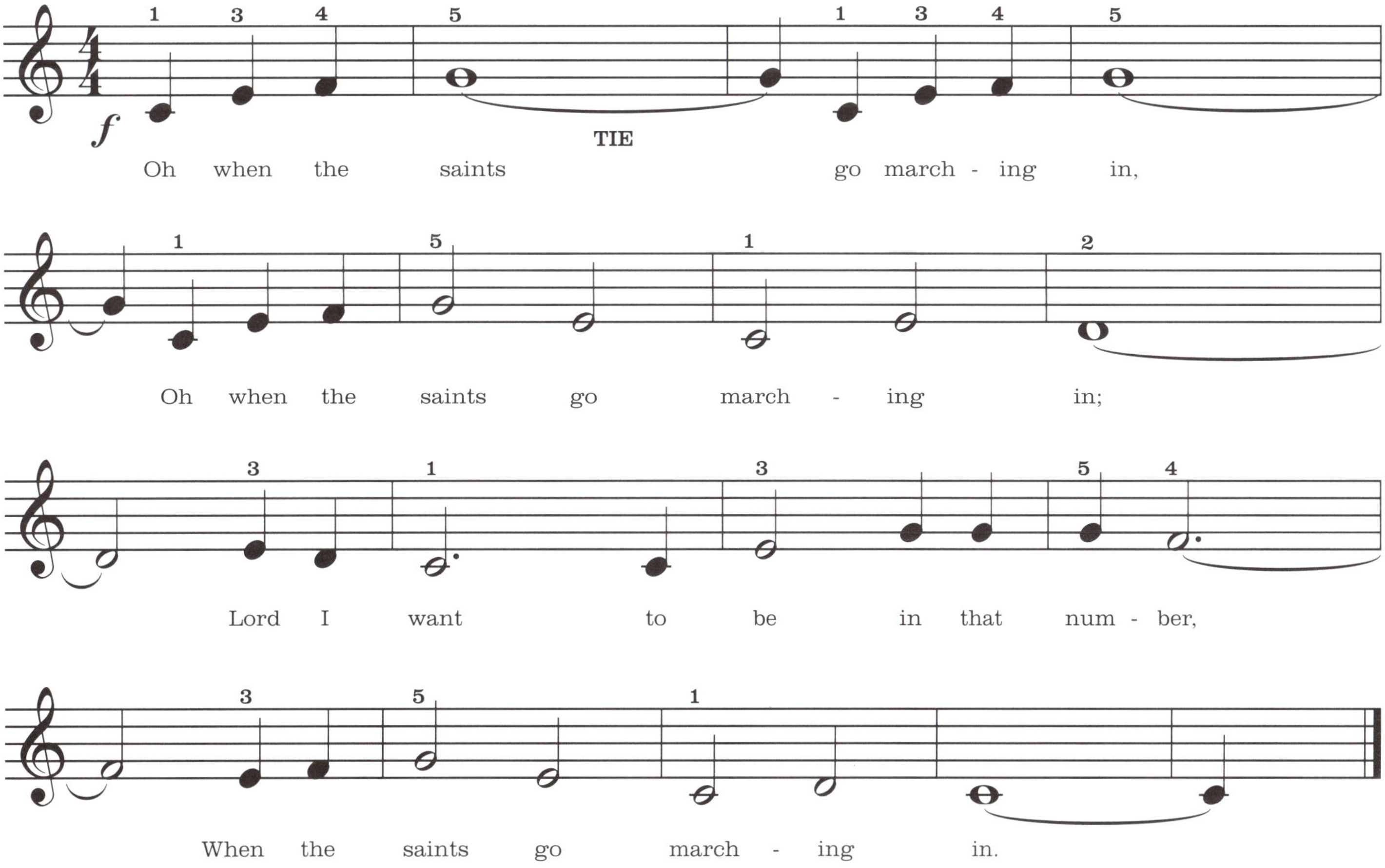
f
TIE
Oh when the saints go march - ing in,
Oh when the saints go march - ing in;
Lord I want to be in that num - ber,
When the saints go march - ing in.

More Exercises For The Little Finger
(R.H.)

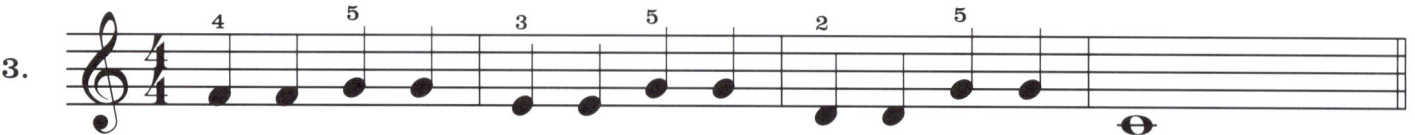

Worksheet 4

1. Give the Italian Term for the following.

    p   (   ) - soft

    f   (   ) - loud

    mf (   ) - moderately loud

    ⌢ - _____

    𝅗𝅥 ⌢ 𝅗𝅥 - _____

2. Circle the correct note.

    Semibreve   ♩   𝅗𝅥   𝅝

    Minim   𝅗𝅥   𝅝   ♩

    Crotchet   𝅝   ♩   𝅗𝅥

3. Write the notes in Semibreves.

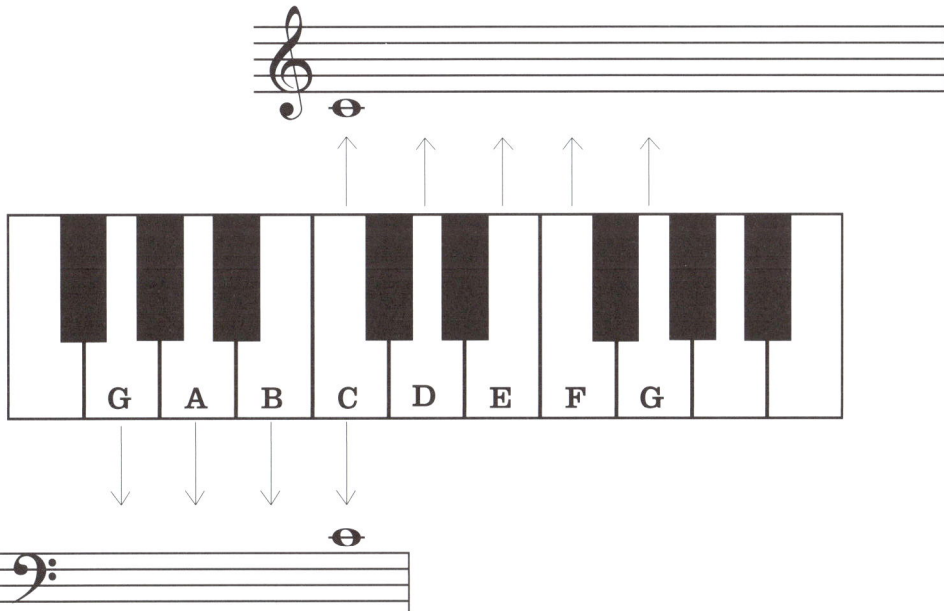

Level 1

Worksheet 5

1. Write the counts: 1 2 3 4

   o   𝅗𝅥   𝅗𝅥.   o   ♩   𝅗𝅥.

   ___   ___   ___   ___   ___   ___

2. Underline the correct answer.

   𝅗𝅥   =   semibreve,   minim,   crotchet,   dotted minim

   𝅗𝅥.   =   semibreve,   minim,   crotchet,   dotted minim

   ♩   =   semibreve,   minim,   crotchet,   dotted minim

   o   =   semibreve,   minim,   crotchet,   dotted minim

3. Name the notes: C D E F G A B

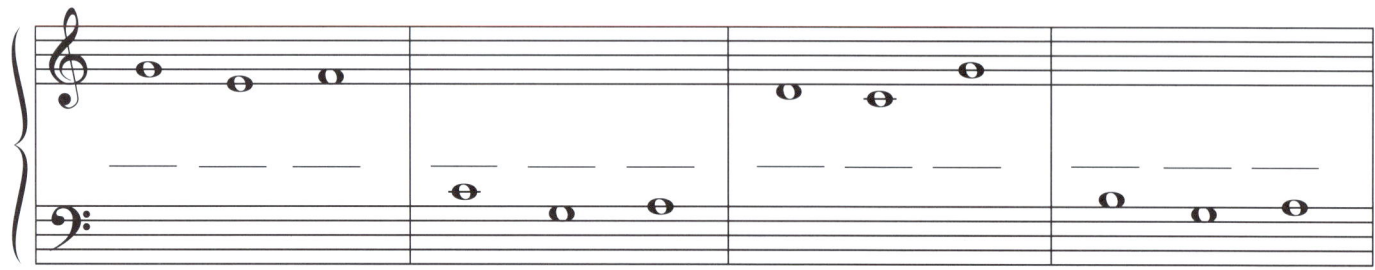

Tempo is the speed of the music.
The tempo here is "Allegro".
It means lively and fast.

Here We Are

Allegro = lively, fast

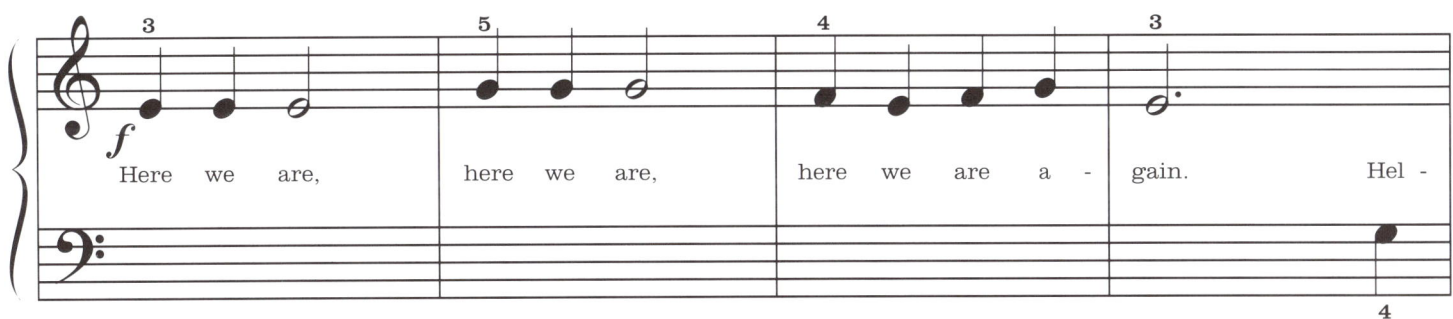

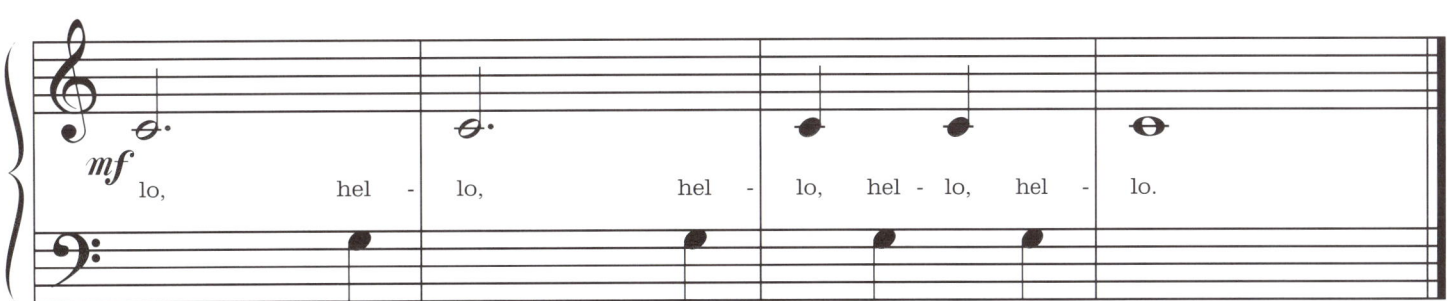

Oral work - What is the tempo of this piece?

What do f and mf stand for?

Level 1

Old MacDonald

Allegro

[Musical score of "Old MacDonald" with lyrics:
"Old Mac-Do-nald had a farm, Ee-ya ee-ya oh, And
on his farm he had some ducks, Ee-ya ee-ya oh.
Quack quack here, quack quack there, Here quack there quack, quack quack quack,
Old Mac-Do-nald had a farm, Ee-ya ee-ya oh."]

Oral work - What is the tempo of this piece? ☐

What is the time signature? ☐

NAME THE SONGS - (1)

Look at the pictures and name the songs orally.

Level 1

Yankee Doodle

Allegretto = slightly slower than **Allegro**

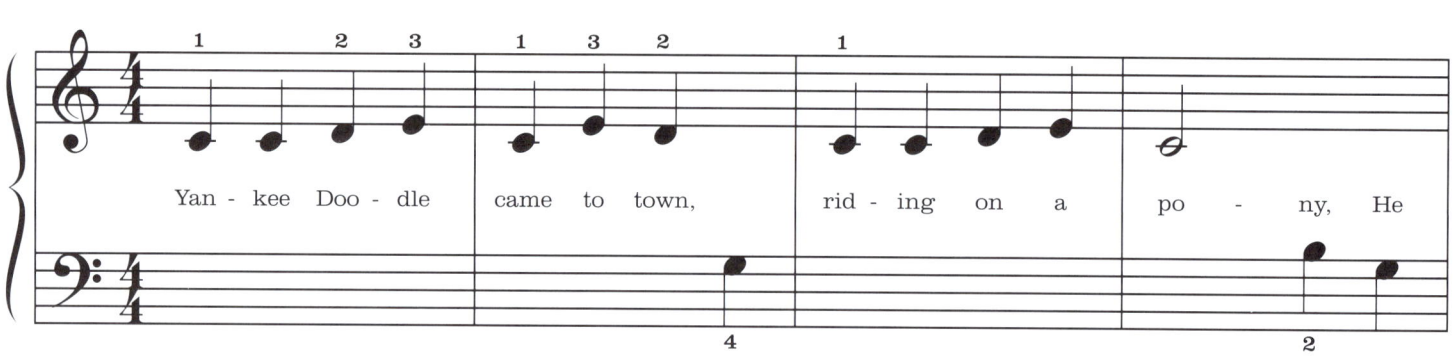

Yan - kee Doo - dle came to town, rid - ing on a po - ny, He

stuck a fea - ther in his cap, and called it Ma - ca - ro - ni.

Oral work - What is the tempo of this piece? ☐

What is the title of the song? ☐

Level 1

Another version: This is the way
　　　　　　　　　I brush my teeth - (3x)
　　　　　　　　　This is the way
　　　　　　　　　I brush my teeth
　　　　　　　　　So early in the morning.

Mulberry Bush

Allegretto

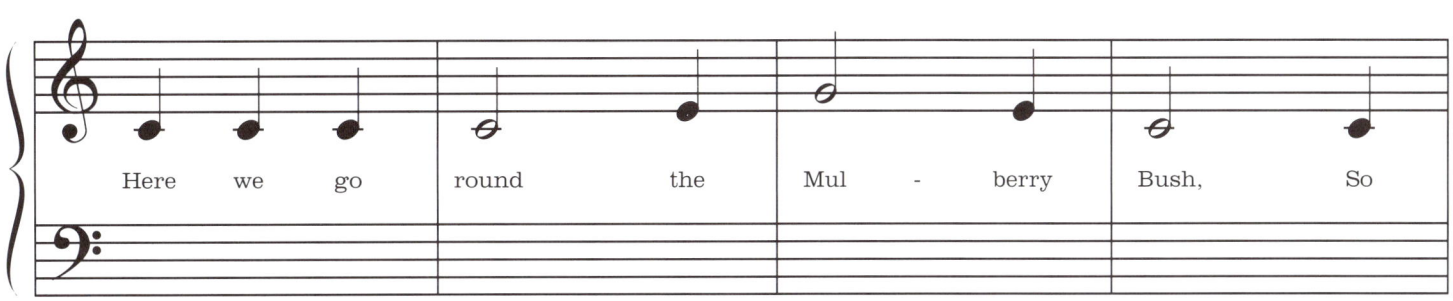

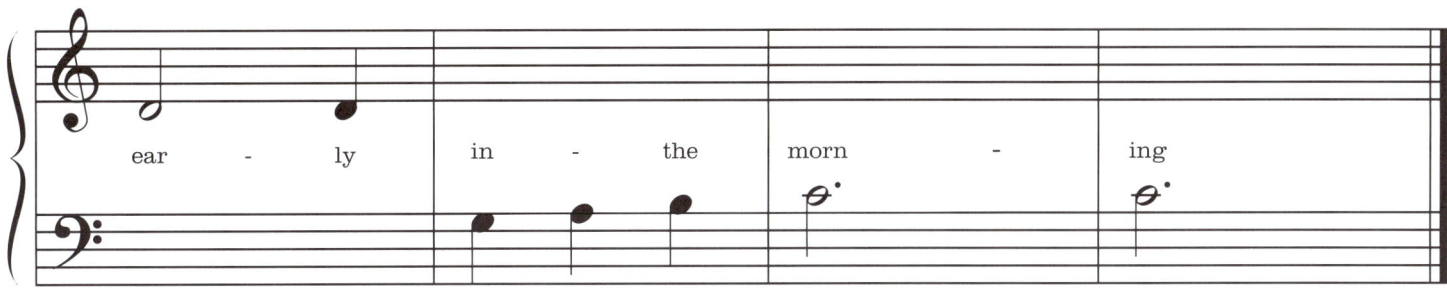

Finger Drill

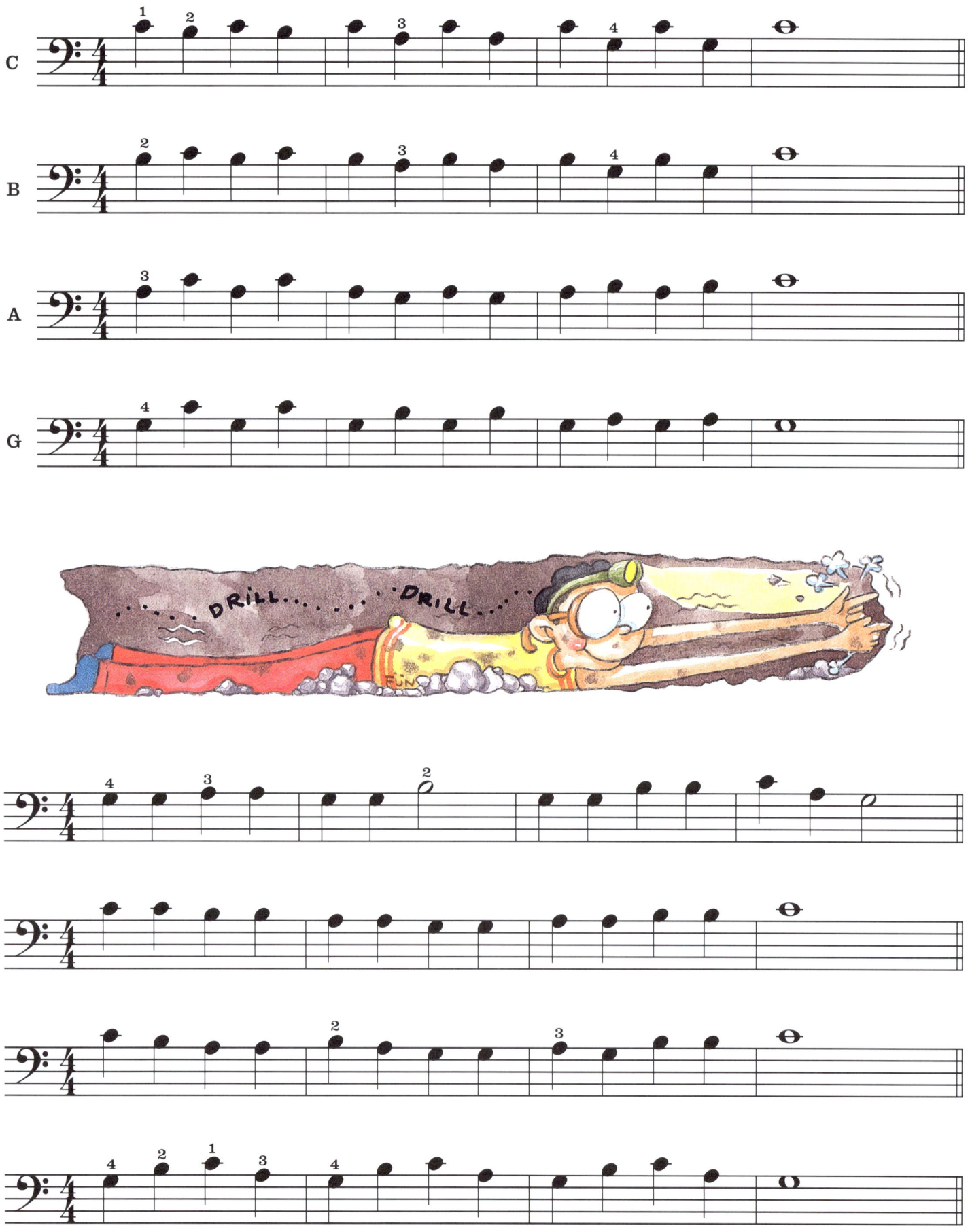

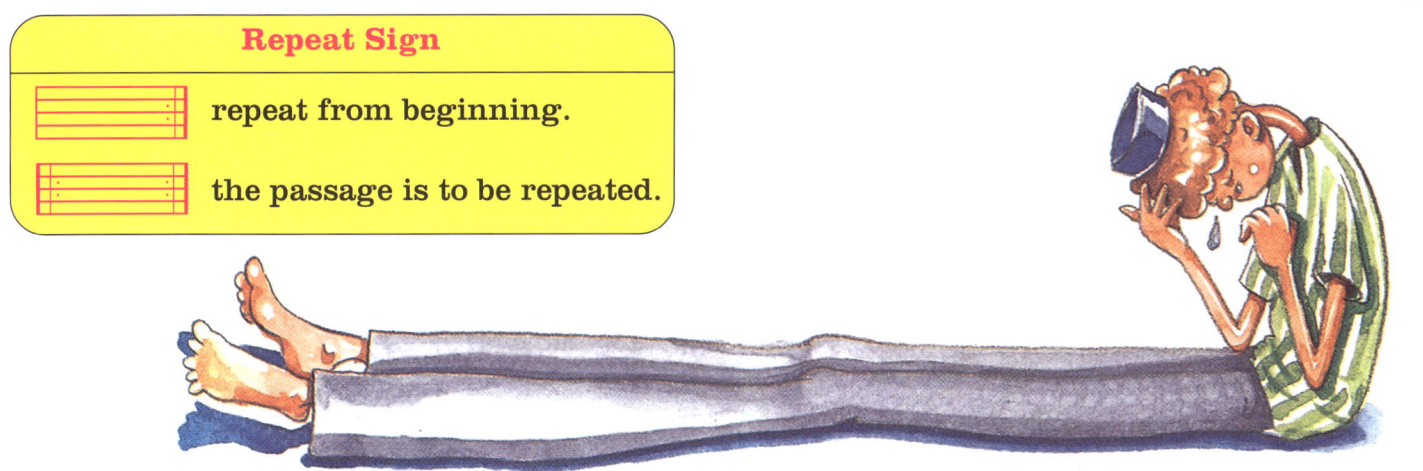

Chan Mali Chan
(Malay Song)

Allegretto

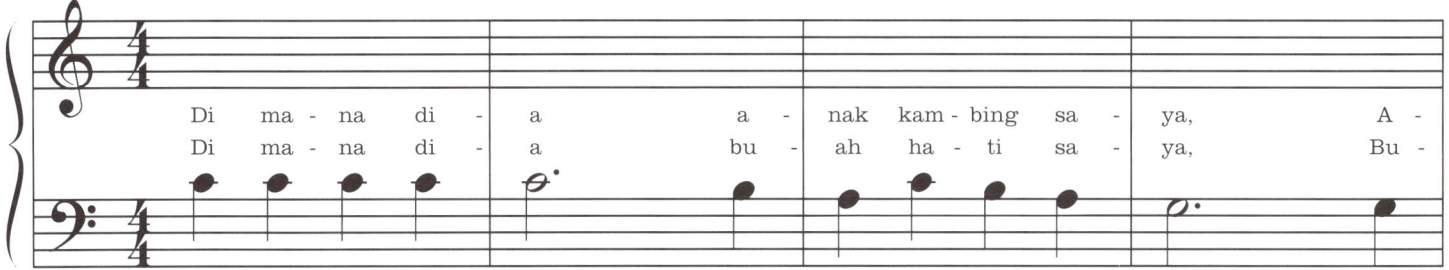

Di ma - na di - a a - nak kam - bing sa - ya, A -
Di ma - na di - a bu - ah ha - ti sa - ya, Bu -

nak kam - bing sa - ya yang ma - kan da - un ta - las.
ah ha - ti sa - ya ba - gai te - lur di ku - pas.

Chan ma - li chan, Chan ma - li chan,

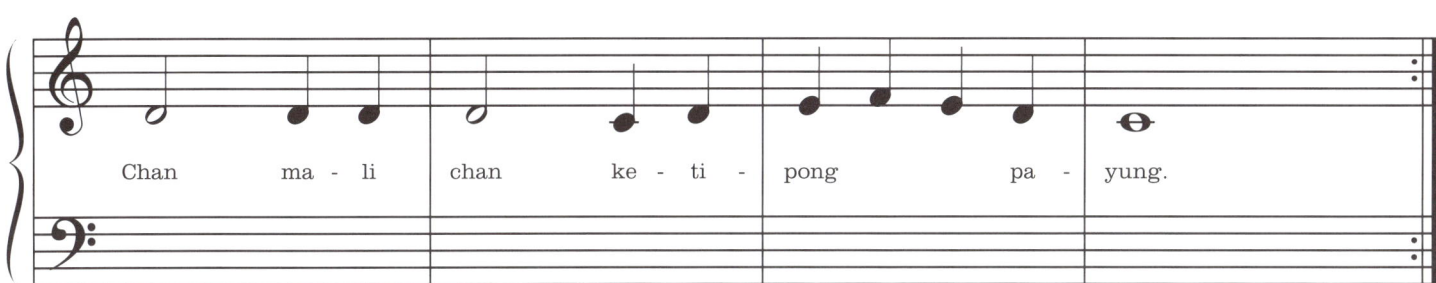

Chan ma - li chan ke - ti - pong pa - yung.

Level 1

mf (mezzo forte) = moderately loud
mp (mezzo piano) = moderately soft

Row Row Row Your Boat

Moderato = moderate speed

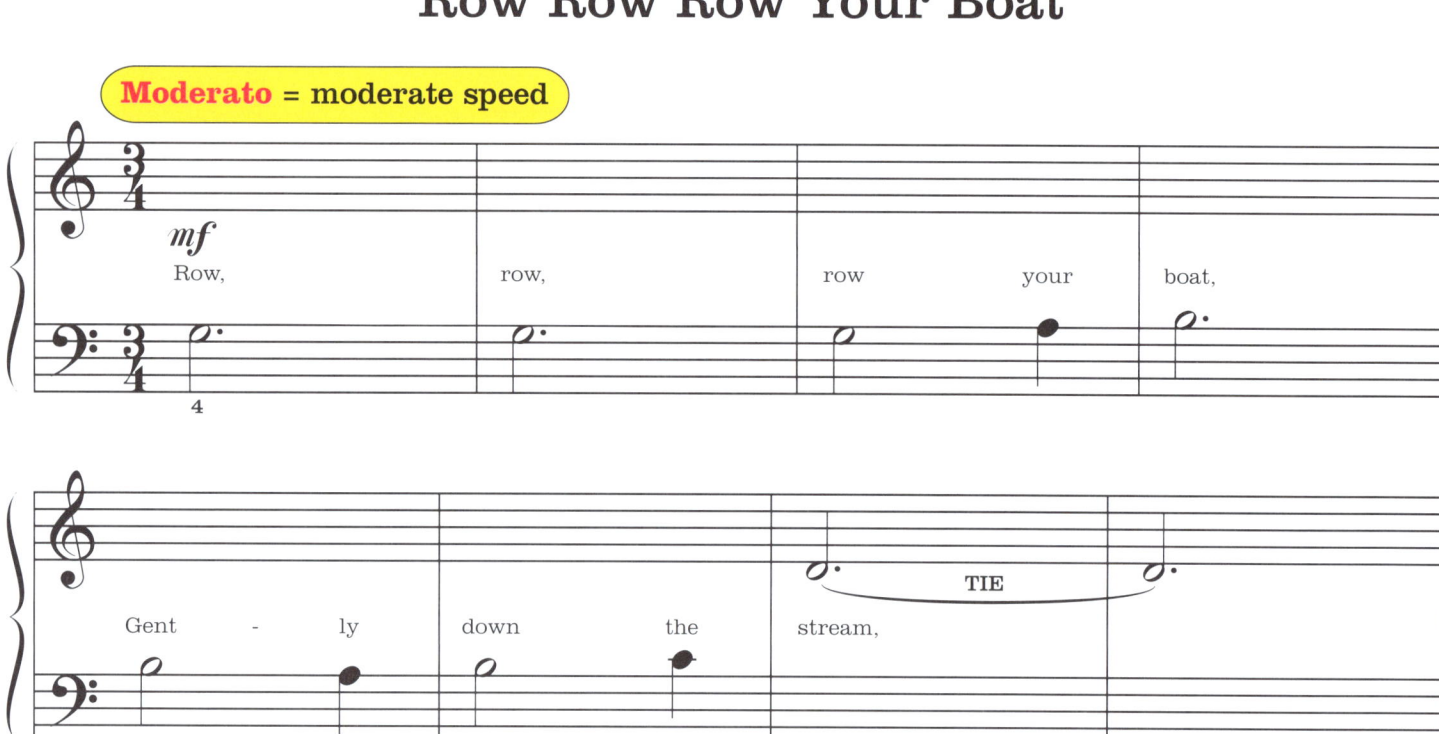

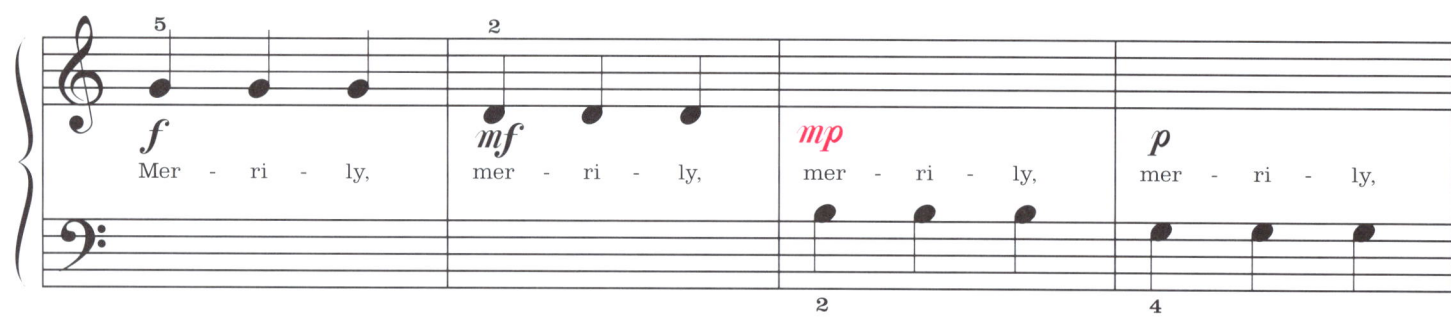

Oral work - Name all the dynamic signs.

Which one is moderate speed - walking or running.

Level 1

WORKSHEET 6

1. Give the meaning of the following.

   Tempo   - _____

   Allegro   - _____

   Allegretto - _____

   Moderato   - _____

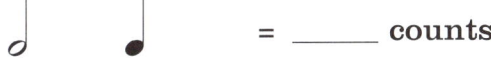

2. Insert the number of counts for the tied notes.

   ♩ ⌣ ♩ = _____ counts   𝅗𝅥 ⌣ 𝅗𝅥 = _____ counts

   𝅝 ⌣ ♩ = _____ counts   𝅗𝅥. ⌣ 𝅗𝅥 = _____ counts

   𝅝 ⌣ 𝅗𝅥 = _____ counts   𝅗𝅥. ⌣ 𝅗𝅥. = _____ counts

3. Insert bar-lines.

Daisy Belle

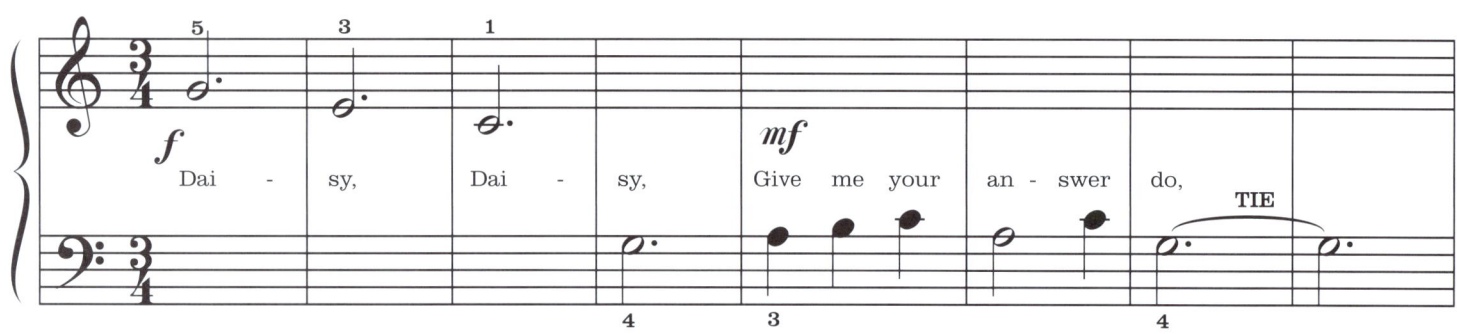
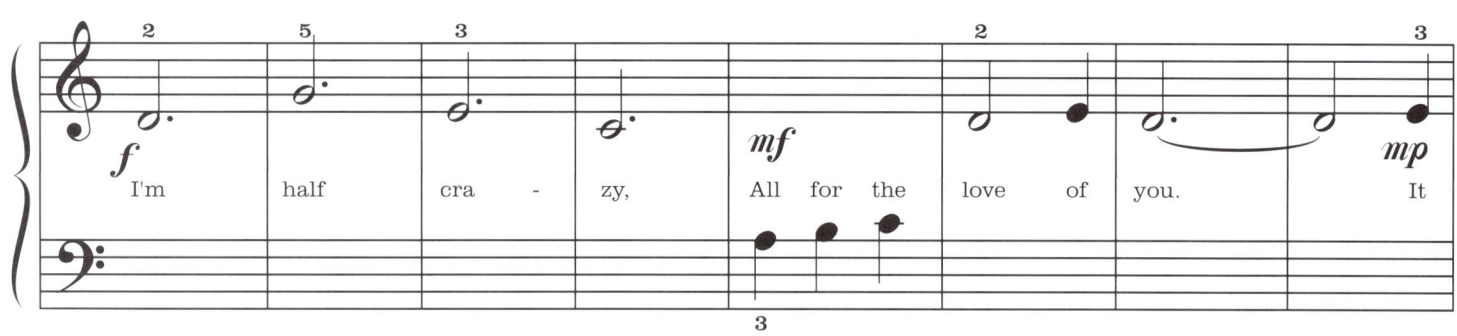
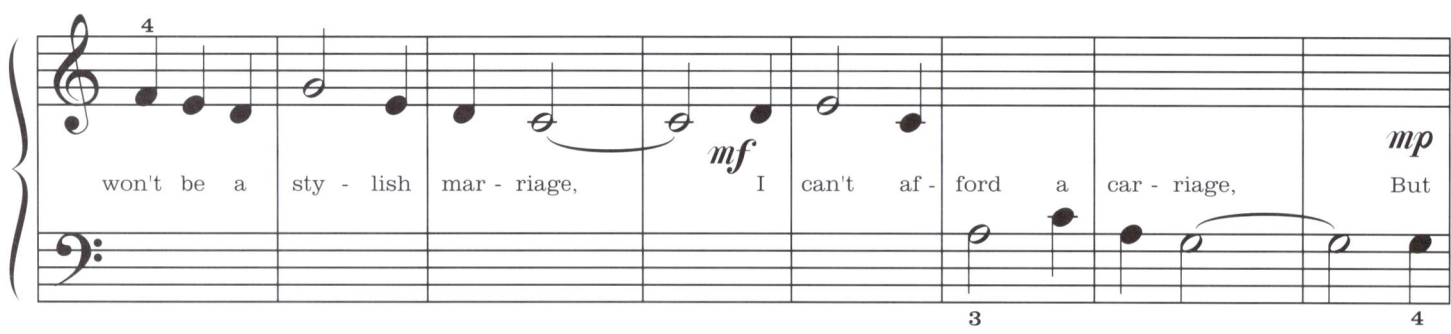
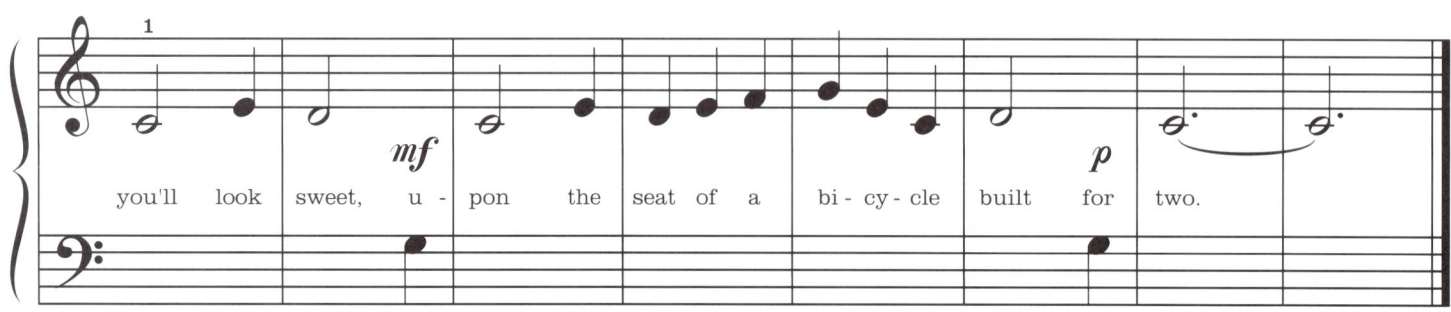

Red River Valley

Lento = slow

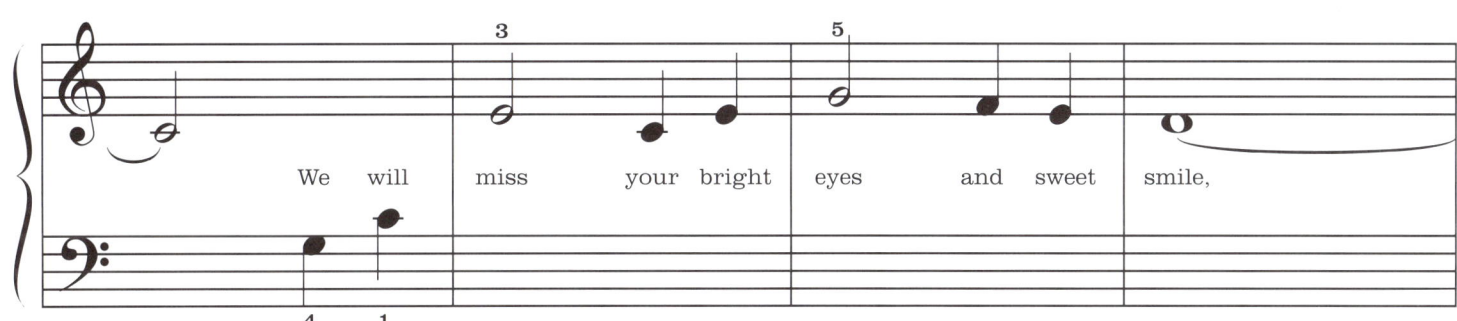

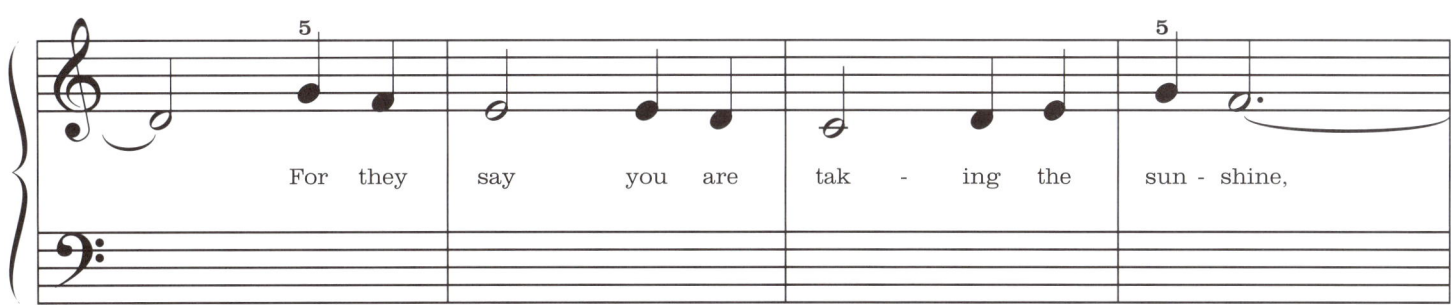

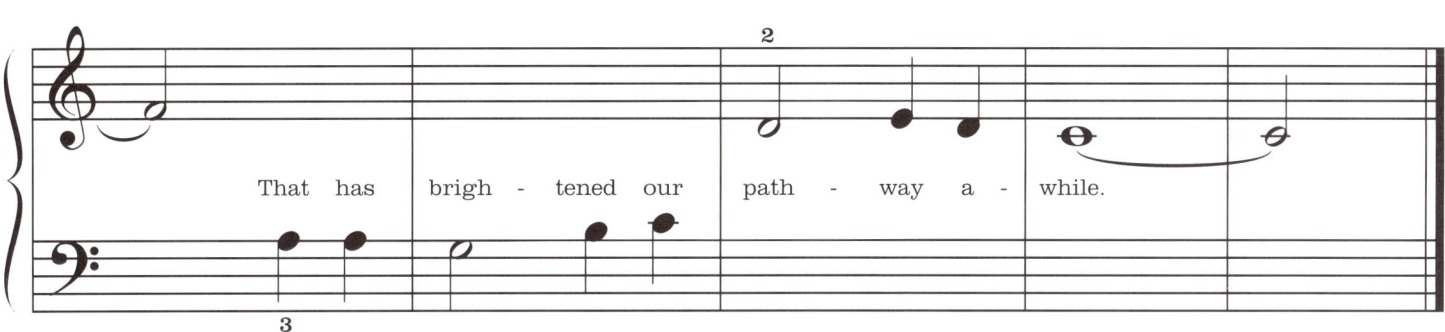

Repeat Sign

 In this case, repeat from beginning.

On Top Of Old Smoky

Moderato

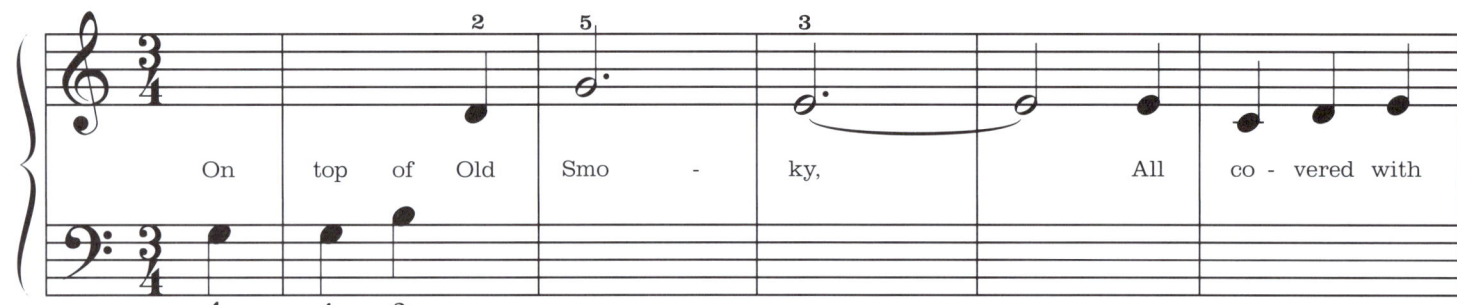

On top of Old Smo - ky, All co - vered with

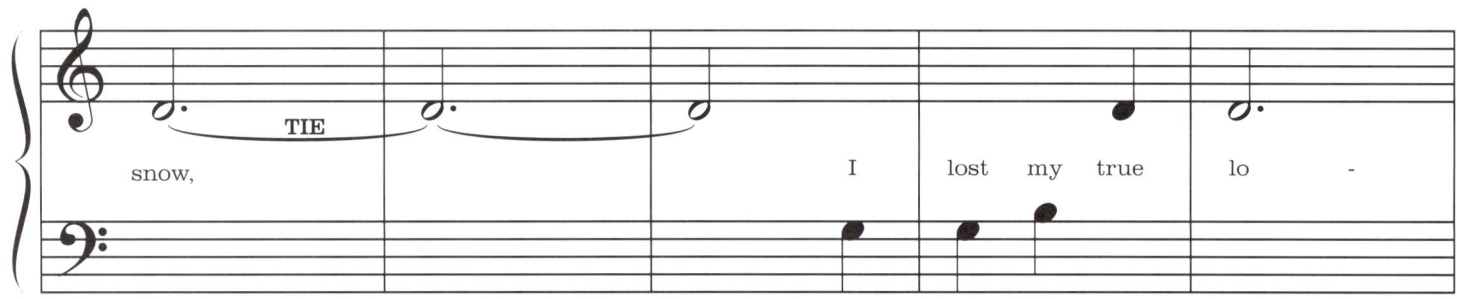

snow, TIE I lost my true lo -

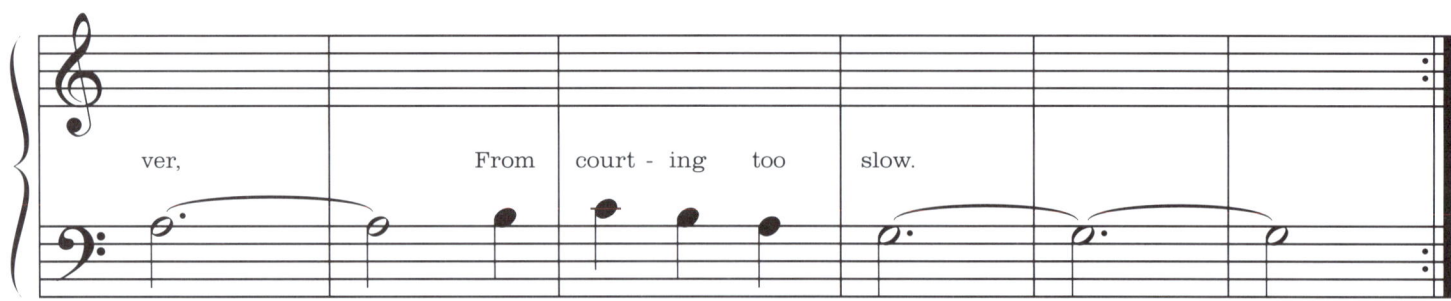

ver, From court - ing too slow.

2nd Verse

For courting's a pleasure
But parting is grief
A false hearted lover
Is worse than a thief.

3rd Verse

A thief he will rob you
And take all you saved
A false hearted lover
Will send you to your grave.

Level 1

Easy Waltz

> **Legato** = is an Italian word. It means smoothly.

WORKSHEET 7

Quaver (♪)

♪ = $\frac{1}{2}$

♫ = ♪ + ♪

= $\frac{1}{2}$ + $\frac{1}{2}$

= 1

1. Colour the pictures using the following colours.
   1 count = red   2 counts = yellow
   3 counts = green   4 counts = orange

2. Insert the counts as shown above.

Level 1

Play and count
(1 and 2 and 3 and 4 and)

Jingle Bells

Allegro = lively, fast

Level 1

Banks Of The Ohio

Lento = slow

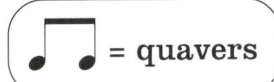 = quavers

Ten Little Indians

Allegretto = slightly slower than **Allegro**

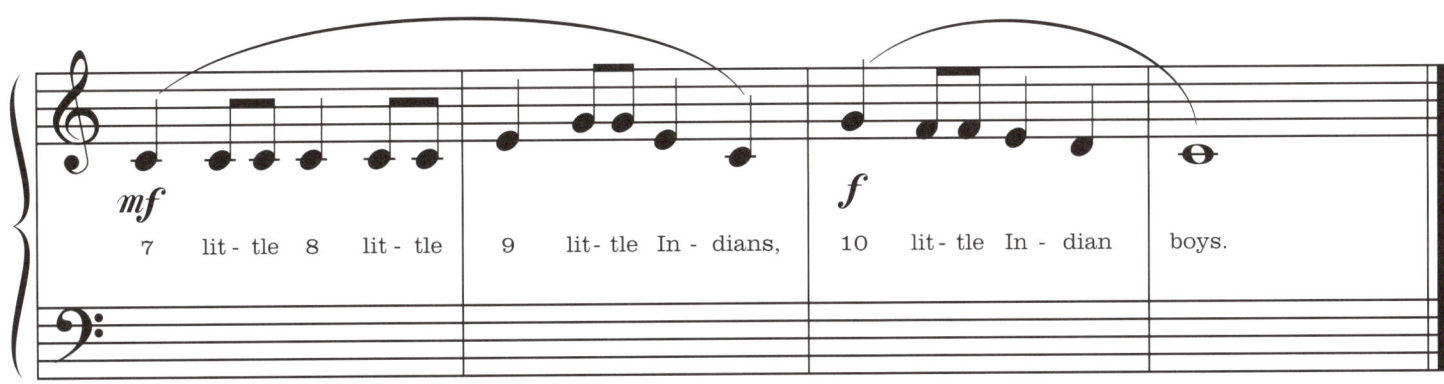

Level 1

This Old Man

Allegretto = slower than **Allegro**

Merry Christmas

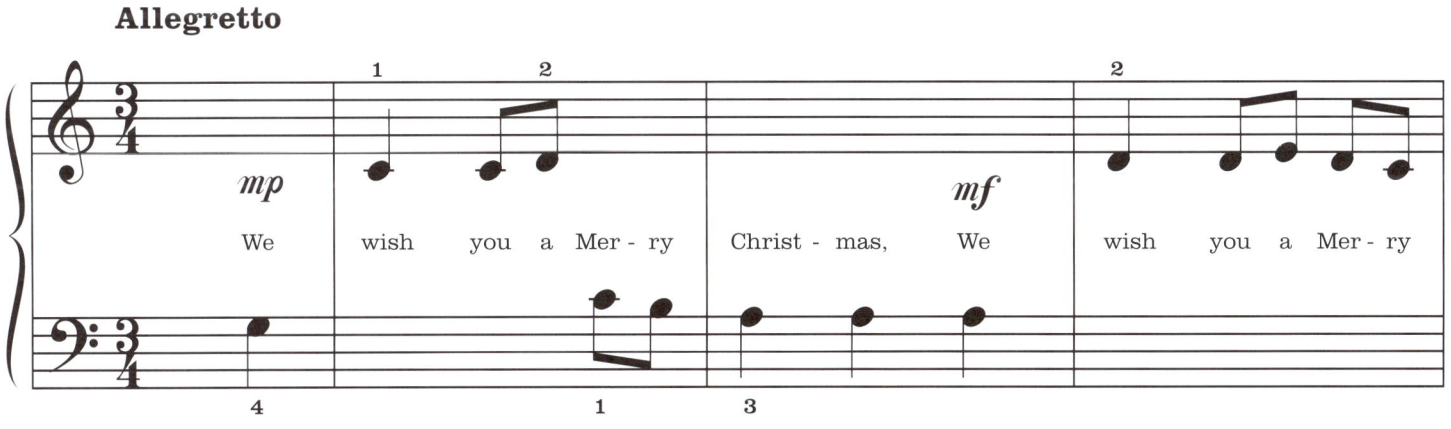
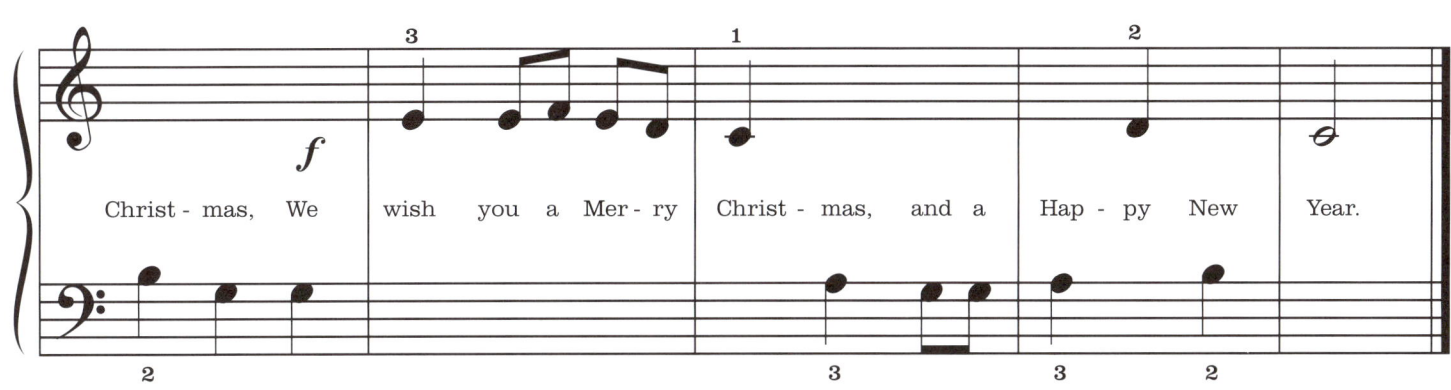

Level 1

Clementine

Moderato = moderate speed

P. Montrose

In a ca-vern, in a can-yon, ex-ca-va-ting for a

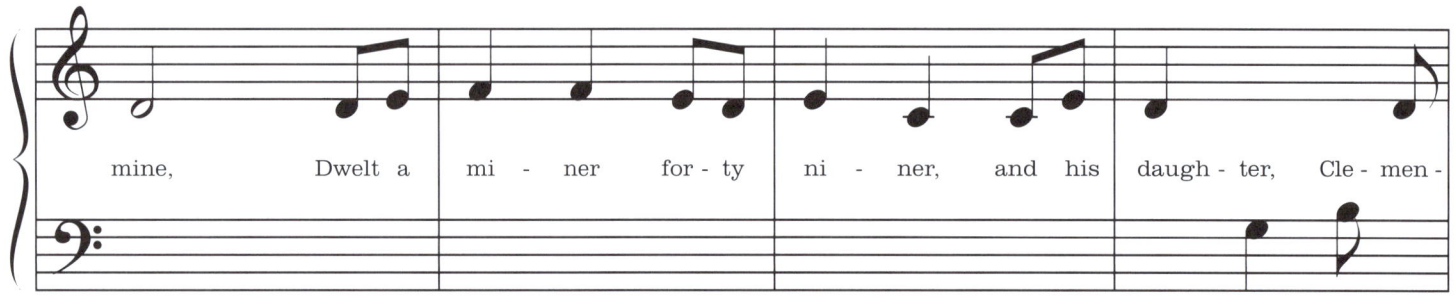

mine, Dwelt a mi-ner for-ty ni-ner, and his daugh-ter, Cle-men-

tine, Oh, my dar-ling, oh, my dar-ling, oh, my dar-ling, Cle-men-

tine, You are lost and gone for-e-ver, dread-ful sor-row, Cle-men-tine.

Level 1

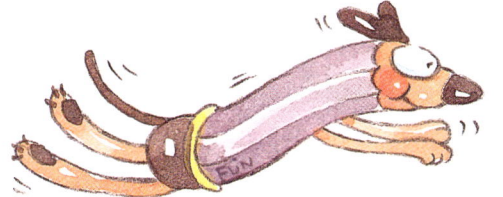

Worksheet 8

Give the meaning of the following.

 - _____

 - _____

 - _____

piano (   ) - _____

forte (   ) - _____

mezzo piano (   ) - _____

mezzo forte (   ) - _____

tempo   - _____

Lento   - _____

Allegro - _____

Allegretto - _____

Moderato - _____

Refer to the page number given and underline the correct answer.

1. How should you play the song in page 31?
   Loudly,   Softly

2. Which tempo is "moderate speed"?
   Allegro,   Allegretto,   Moderato

3. What is the tempo in page 41?
   Allegro,   Allegretto,   Moderato

4. What new sign can you find in page 41?
   ||: :|| ,   *mp* ,   *mf*

5. Which one is a lively song?
   Here We Are (35),   Row Your Boat (42),   Red River Valley (45)

6. Which tempo is slow?
   Allegro,   Moderato,   Lento

Level 1

NAME THE SONGS - (2)

Look at the pictures and name the songs orally.